D1336859

04589734

PLANTS

E**X**TREME FACTS

BY ROBIN TWIDDY

©2019
The Secret Book
Company
King's Lynn
Norfolk PE30 4LS

ISBN: 978-1-912502-02-8

Written by:
Robin Twiddy
Edited by:
Madeline Tyler
Designed by:
Jasmine Pointer

A catalogue record for this book
is available from the British Library

PHOTO CREDITS

Front cover – DRogatnev, Panda Vector, Gabi Wolf, Maike Hildebrandy, MicroOne.
4 – Anna Koshelev, Elegant Solution. 5 – Panda Vector. 6 – Amanita Silvicora,
Iconic Bestiary, Soyon, Dzm1try. 7 – solmariart, Zefir, notbad. 8 – Natali Snailcat,
Michele Paccione, drical. 9 – ALD Materials, light_s. Julia's Art, NotionPic. 10 –
Macrovector, KoDi Art, Yana Alisovna, Visual Generation, SilviaC, Sarycheva Olesia,
Abdie, DRogatnev, Ilya Bolotov, Dim Tik. 11 – Alekseeva Yulia, Jakinnboaz, Flying
Master, Miroslava Hlavacova. 12 – labzazuza, Sentavio, Chalintra.B, BigMouse,
Nosyrevy. 13 – SaveJungle, VectorPixelStar, 14 – iana kauri, , Angyee Patipat,
TaniaLudz, HannaVector, Daria Riabets, KsanaGraphica. 15 – barkarola, Anatolir,
LynxVector, Nataliia Zhydchenko, Hanaha. 16 – Lemberg Vector studio, Jamesbin.
17 – VikiVector, AVA Bitter, MuchMania, Orakunya, LineTale. 18 – ju.hrozian, AMY LI,
Rvector, AnnstasAg, LRSGA72. 19 – Toltemara, Lemberg Vector studio, avtor painter.
20 – BigMouse, Artlusy, MicroOne, robuart, Nanashiro, Aayam 4D. 21 – KittyVector,
lovesiyu, marselparis, Maluson. 22 – stockakia, VFilimonov, moj0j0, Viktoriya Belova.
23 – MatiasDelCarmine, Rvector, VectorShow.

Images are courtesy of Shutterstock.com. With thanks to Getty Images, Thinkstock
Photo and iStockphoto.

CONTENTS

Page 4   Parts of a Plant
Page 6   Grass
Page 8   Plants
Page 10   Flowers
Page 12   Trees
Page 14   Seeds
Page 16   Rainforests
Page 18   Deserts
Page 20   Underwater
Page 22   Deadly
Page 24   Glossary and Index

Words that look like <u>this</u> can be found in the glossary on page 24.

PARTS OF A PLANT

Plants are amazing things that make up around 82 percent (%) of all life on Earth. But what makes up a plant?

STEM

The stem carries water and nutrients up from the roots to the other parts of the plant. It also helps bring the flower and leaves closer to light <u>sources</u>.

ROOTS

The roots of a plant are usually found underground and take up water and <u>nutrients</u> from the soil.

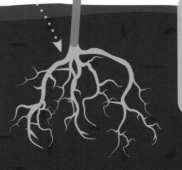

The deepest roots ever recorded belonged to the shepherd tree, reaching 68 metres underground.

Some plants, such as potatoes, have stems that grow underground.

FLOWERS

The flower is the part of the plant that holds the <u>reproductive organs</u>. Flowers make seeds that can make new plants.

Most flowers need insects or other creatures to help them <u>pollinate,</u> but some flowers can self-pollinate.

LEAVES

Leaves are the part of the plant that trap energy from the Sun.

The largest leaf in the world belongs to the raffia palm tree. Some leaves can grow up to 21 metres long. That is about the length of four cars!

GRASS

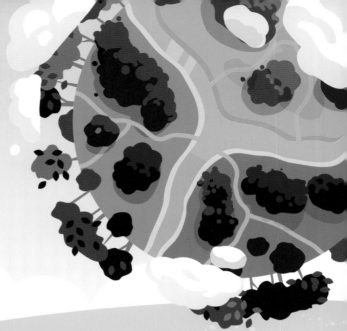

About 25% of the Earth's land is covered in grass.

There are around 12,000 known <u>species</u> of grass.

Bamboo is a type of grass.

Bamboo grows more quickly than any other plant. The fastest-growing species can grow up to 91 centimetres (cm) per day.

The oldest living thing on the planet is a sea grass found in the Mediterranean Sea. It is believed to be 200,000 years old.

Wheat, corn and rice are all part of the grass family.

Palm trees are more closely <u>related</u> to grass than to oak trees.

Some scientists believe that the smell of freshly cut grass is the grass plant warning other grass of danger.

PLANTS

Ferns were around long before the dinosaurs.

There are more than 80,000 plant species on Earth that we can eat.

Animal poo, known as manure, helps plants to grow.

Different poos are better for different plants.

There are over **200,000** known plant species.

Just **30 species of plant** provide **90%** of the foods that humans eat.

Scientists have made a burger that looks, tastes, smells and cooks just like meat, but is made completely from plants. It even bleeds!

The science of studying plants is called botany.

9

FLOWERS

Flowers did not always exist. **They appeared some time around 130 million years ago.**

The corpse flower gets its name from the smell it gives off when it is in <u>**bloom**</u>. It smells like a rotting body!

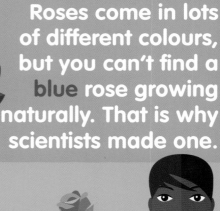

Roses come in lots of different colours, but you can't find a blue rose growing naturally. That is why scientists made one.

There was a time in Holland when **tulip bulbs** were more valuable than gold.

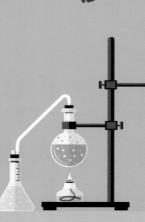

Broccoli is actually a flower. We <u>harvest</u> and eat it before it flowers.

Most flowers have both male and female **reproductive parts.**

Stigma (female)

Stamen (male)

The most expensive flower in the world is the Kadupul flower. It dies almost as soon as it is picked.

Some **orchids** do not need soil to live in. They can grow hanging from trees.

TREES

If cut, the dragon blood tree 'bleeds' a red resin. This is where the tree gets its name from.

The oldest tree in the world is thought to be a 9,550-year-old spruce tree in Sweden.

The tallest tree in the world can be found in California. The coast redwood named Hyperion is an amazing 115 metres tall.

The rainbow eucalyptus tree has the most colourful trunk on Earth. It produces bright green stripes of sap that change colour as they dry.

Trees can help prevent floods. When there is heavy rain, trees can absorb <u>excess</u> water before it reaches drains or rivers.

99% of a living tree is dead. The only parts that are alive are the leaves, buds, root tips and a thin layer under the bark.

You can tell how old a tree is by studying its growth rings. Each ring is a year. This is called dendrochronology.

The largest mammal that lives in trees is the orangutan.

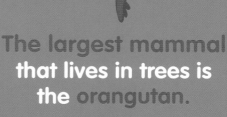

13

SEEDS

The biggest seed in the world comes from the coco de mer tree. It has a <u>diameter</u> of 50 cm and can weigh up to 25 kilograms. That's almost as heavy as a fully grown Labrador!

The smallest seed in the world belongs to a certain type of orchid. This orchid produces seeds that are so small that you might think that they are dust.

Animals spread plant seeds that are found in their poo after eating fruits containing the seeds.

Some plants need the heat from <u>wildfires</u> to crack open their fruit and release the seeds so that they can grow into new plants.

The world's largest seed bank, known as the 'Doomsday Vault', is the Svalbard Global Seed Vault located in the Arctic Circle. It holds more than 980,000 seeds.

Most dandelion seeds land within ten metres of the <u>parent plant</u>. However, with the right conditions, they can travel up to a kilometre.

Some seeds, such as those of the burdock plant, travel by attaching themselves to animal fur using tiny hooks.

Harvester ants collect and plant seeds. When the seed breaks open and begins to grow, the ants eat what is inside.

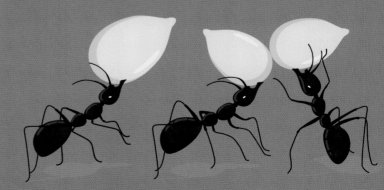

RAINFORESTS

Rainforests cover only 6% of the Earth's surface, but they contain over half of all plant and animal species in the world!

The <u>canopy</u> of the rainforest can be so thick that it can take up to ten minutes for a raindrop to make it to the ground.

One tree in the rainforest can have more than 40 species of ant on and in it. That is more than all the species of ants in Britain.

Around 20% of the world's oxygen comes from the plants in the Amazon rainforest.

70% of the plants used to treat cancer are found only in rainforests.

The Amazon rainforest is home to an estimated **40,000** species of plant.

It is estimated that over 32,375 hectares of rainforest are being destroyed every day.

Things <u>decompose</u> up to **ten times** quicker in rainforests than in other <u>biomes</u>.

DESERTS

There is more plant life in the desert than you might expect. The Sonoran Desert is home to around 2,500 different species of plant.

The Welwitschia mirabilis, also known as the desert onion, can live to over 1,500 years old.

The peccary, which is a pig-like animal, has <u>evolved</u> a tough mouth and <u>digestive system</u>. This is so it can eat prickly pear cactus plants without getting pricked by thousands of spines.

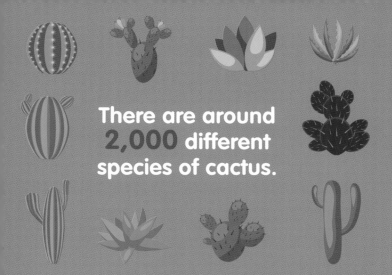

There are around **2,000 different species of cactus.**

Some cacti have spines instead of leaves. Spines lose less water than leaves, making them better suited for hot areas.

Cacti can survive from **15 to 300 years** depending on the type of cactus.

The saguaro cactus can grow to around **18 metres tall.**

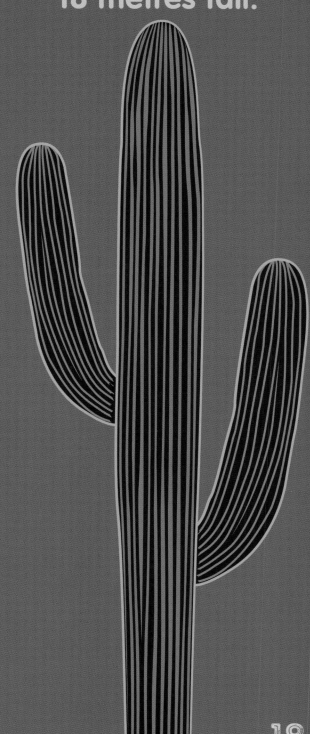

UNDERWATER

85% of plant life on Earth is found in the ocean.

Unlike land plants, some <u>aquatic</u> plants' roots are not attached to anything and the plants float freely around the ocean.

Coral is not a plant. It is the algae that gives it its amazing colours. The algae and coral have a symbiotic relationship. This means that they need and help each other.

Aquatic plants release oxygen into the water, helping animals such as fish to live there.

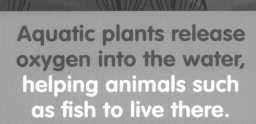

For a long time, scientists believed that plants in the ocean could only grow as deep as 210 metres below the surface. When they found algae growing 274 metres below the surface, they knew this wasn't true!

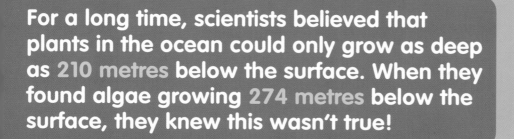

Pyrodinium is a type of <u>phytoplankton</u> that glows bright blue when it is disturbed.

Seagrass is the only completely <u>submerged</u> saltwater plant that produces flowers.

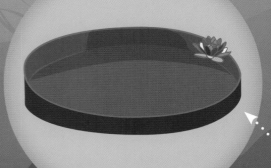

The giant Amazon water lily can grow a floating pad that is usually between 60 and 180 cm in diameter.

DEADLY

Deadly nightshade has sweet berries that, if eaten, can stop your heart from beating and kill you.

The angel's trumpet flower is <u>poisonous</u>. Eating it can make you confused, very thirsty and nervous. Your heart will beat faster until you die. Don't eat the angel's trumpet!

Nepenthes rajah is a species of pitcher plant. It is the largest meat-eating plant in the world. It is big enough to trap and eat rats, but it prefers tree shrew poo.

Dendrocnide moroides, also known as gympie gympie, has the most painful sting of any plant. After being stung, the skin becomes red and <u>swollen</u> and people can feel the pain for months.

Hemlock was the flower used to make the poison that killed the famous Greek <u>philosopher</u> and teacher Socrates in 399 BC.

Aconitum, also known as monkshood or wolfsbane, contains a poison in its roots and leaves that can cause vomiting and diarrhoea, and sometimes death. Some archers used to dip their arrows in the poison.

In the 19th century there were several reports of trees eating people in and around the continent of Africa. These turned out to be a <u>hoax</u>.

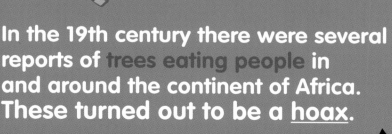

GLOSSARY

aquatic	living or growing near to or in water
biomes	natural areas, home to a community of plants and animals
bloom	to flower or blossom
canopy	the top layer of plant life in a jungle, which creates a roof-like area above the trees
decompose	to decay and rot
diameter	the distance through the centre of a circle or sphere
digestive system	the parts of the body that work together to break down food
evolved	slowly developed and adapted to an environment over a long time
excess	more than the needed amount
harvest	collect or gather something that has grown, such as crops
hoax	an act or story meant to trick someone
nutrients	natural substances that are needed for plants to grow
parent plant	the plant that provided the seed for another plant
philosopher	a person who studies the nature of knowledge, reality and existence
phytoplankton	tiny plant-like things that are found in water, such as algae
poisonous	dangerous or deadly when eaten
pollinate	move pollen from one flower to another
related	having a connection to
reproductive organs	the parts of an animal or plant that allow it to make new members of its species
sources	where things come from
species	a group of very similar animals or plants that are capable of producing young together
submerged	completely underwater
swollen	to become larger in size because of growth or pressure
wildfires	fires, usually in natural surroundings, that burn quickly and uncontrollably

INDEX

Amazon 16–17, 21

cacti 18–19

coral 20

deserts 18–19

Earth 4, 8, 13, 16, 20

flowers 4–5, 10–11, 21–23

food 9

fruit 14

leaves 4–5, 13–14, 19, 23

oxygen 16, 20

poo 8, 14, 22

rainforests 16–17

roots 4, 13, 20, 23

scientists 7, 9–10, 21

seeds 5, 14–15

Socrates 23

Sonoran desert 18

stem 4, 18

trees 4–5, 7, 11–14, 16, 22–23